MENTALLY TOUGH IN A WEAK SOCIETY

MITCHELL TUCKER

DEDICATION

I dedicate this book to my parents, Ken & Bobbi Tucker. I love you two very much and I am so very grateful that you instilled in me from a young age what it meant to be mentally TOUGH!

TABLE OF CONTENTS

PREFACE

The definition of mental toughness may be different depending on who you ask. You know, one of the things that qualifies us as humans is our ability to think and process information differently. It has been said that, when many people are thinking the same thing, no one is actually thinking.

Read this first page and determine what it means to you before you continue. As you go through the book, keep a mental note as to your definition. This will only help further embrace and build the mindset you need to be mentally tough!

Webster describes "Mental" as: "specifically: of or relating to the total emotional and intellectual response of an individual to external reality" and toughness as: "Capable of enduring strain, hardship, or severe labor." So, when looking at the phrase "Mentally Tough" or "Mentally Strong", we think of someone who essentially is strong enough emotionally to endure or get through hard times. Someone who has developed a resilient system that enables him/her to endure every experience without much emotional agony. Someone who can clear the fog off his/her mind when things are tough, without much labor. Looking around society today, it occurs to me that only few are in possession of the mental toughness I mentioned earlier. I see that, when I look around, there are many more people who would rather give up than repeat or even modify a failed process. I feel our society is slowly losing our mental toughness. This is somewhat of a propellant for me to write this book. So, I hope to keep you entertained long enough to bring to life that already deadened mental strength in you. I'll begin this by showing you some awesome examples of men and women who have the ultimate level of mental toughness and show you how you can begin to demonstrate the same characteristics.

As we go through this book, I want you to take note of the different individuals we meet, their mentality, and their ability to endure what most would consider impossible. We all deal with stress and frustration in some form or another, and we all handle it differently. Stress and frustration can be induced by finances, medical situations, relationships, and so much more. To quote one of my heroes, as he laid on a hospital bed with his heart failing: "Son, you have to stress the big stuff, this isn't big." -Ken Tucker. When I heard my dad say that, I couldn't help but laugh with anxiety, but then the reality slapped me in the face. How can I cave under pressure and stress over superficial things when he considers his "heart failing" not a big thing? This mental toughness is what makes average men and women into millionaires, people of influence, known artists, great parents, and essentially anything they set their minds to be.

I was fortunate to have a mother and father who are both mentally tough. As a side note, mentally tough does not mean emotionless. You can be a mental ninja and hold a child's hand, cry with a friend, and treat people with compassion. But when you take a shot that would crush others, you stand up and laugh at adversity.

Sorry for the cliché reference, but I must reference the movie *300*. This movie demonstrates physical toughness, but too often, that is all we focus on. The illusion in this world of ours is that physical ability charges up mental ability. We often believe that one needs to be very physically strong to succeed, especially in businesses. On the contrary, however, the extent of your mental toughness is what propels your physical force.

The mental toughness that these men demonstrated when standing against an army of 100k to 150k men was incredible. I can't vouch for the accuracy of this movie, but I can say the mental toughness that the director was able to depict was awesome! I encourage you to take a moment and think of someone you admire. The achievements they have been able to obtain and the obstacles they have overcome. Often, we look at these people and think of how strong, talented or smart they may be, but we fail to recognize the mentality it took to take that attribute to a level where they are recognized for it. Sports were a big part of my life growing up, and when you study the greats, you can see how their mentality played a HUGE role in them being successful. The following are quotes from some of the greats in their industry and show exactly what their mentality looked like:

"If you run into a wall don't turn around and give up. Figure out how to climb it, go through it, or work around it."
-Michael Jordan

"If my mind can conceive it and my heart can believe it – Then I can achieve it."
-Muhammad Ali

"You can't put a limit on anything, the more you dream the further you get."
-Michael Phelps

"No matter how far you get ahead of me. I'm going to catch you, that's my mentality."

-Usain Bolt

"You wanna know which ring is my favorite? The next one."

-Tom Brady

"The more you play baseball, the less depends on your athletic ability. It's a mental war more than anything."

-Alex Rodriguez

"Before you can achieve, you must believe in yourself."

-Mike Trout

There could be an entire book of quotes. I just wanted to share a few that I thought stood out and help share the mentality of some of these athletes.

This same mentality can be used in business, health, relationships, finances etc. Determine your WHY and brace yourself because things are not always fair, and life is not easy...

CHAPTER I
THE ESSENCE OF MENTAL TOUGHNESS

I envision this book to be a book that answers the most disturbing questions regarding our mentality. Really, we have been continuously asking ourselves questions for a while, and I think it is important to share my own working principles, or if you like, my own answers to the questions. I see this more as an obligation for me as I have a burning desire to see everyone hit their goals and succeed!

I want to start this chapter by saying, what differentiates humans from animals is the superiority of their thinking. Although when placed side by side with these animals, plants and insects, the number of living humans is minuscule. Not too surprisingly, however, humans control every other living thing. It is obvious then to see the reason humans are referred to as "higher animals" by biologists. Humans always see the need to improve their present states. They always try to challenge themselves to make things better and do things more easily. And certainly, man has come a very long way from the first hunting tools to artificial intelligence . . . While of course, that is not the basis of this book (as I am no biology professor), it is important to point out the usefulness of the mental in the improvement of the physical.

The truth of the matter, as we have come to realize it, is that even among humans, there are those who are much more mentally healthy than others. And that is what brings this broad topic into full view. So, if I would take my license here, I would classify humans into two groups based on their mental state. On one hand, we have the mentally weak people, (or average rather) and on the other hand, we have the mentally tough. We could also say we have the weak breed and the tough breed. And we know that whatever is described as 'tough' or 'strong' is superior to that which is termed 'weak' or 'feeble'. But how do we know which side of the coin we belong to? What differentiates the mentally weak from the mentally strong? I would like you to picture a story with me in your mind where we can draw inferences with which I hope to answer these questions.

Imagine a boy was sent to deliver a package to his father's friend down the street. On the way, he discovers the package is missing.

As humans, we have the tendency to react in every situation. Now to our assessment. The first thing that came to my mind in this scenario would be another series of questions: How did it get lost? What did the boy do? And there are many variables we could get. Did he sit down and start crying? Did he turn right back and search for it? Did he proceed to his destination to explain his ordeal? Or did he run away?

While I would say the option the boy picks is not what tells if he is mentally tough or not, I would like to think it is a guide into the mental chart of the boy. We could infer that, if he sits and cries, he is ashamed of his failure. If he begins looking for the package, that tells us he is proactive. We could also guess the boy is afraid if he runs away.

What brings mental toughness into full view is what experience the boy gains from the situation. Always remember that NOTHING IS EVER TOUGH OR WEAK UNTIL IT HAS BEEN TESTED. So, we would ask further questions to answer the initial question of who is mentally tough and who is not taking the example of the boy as a case study. The one question we would ask this time is: how did he improve himself based on that experience? (Let's consider that he chooses any of the options and gets scolded.)

The answer we get from that question is what brings us to a definite conclusion of who is tough mentally and who isn't. The mentally tough would learn from that mistake and become more careful, while on the other hand, the mentally weak would become even more afraid of being sent on such errands. From this illustration, I come to the conclusion that EXPERIENCE is a key determinant factor in the making of the mentally weak and the mentally tough. The journey of being mentally tough or weak begins when you make your first mistake. So, tell me, who doesn't make mistakes? Imagine yourself travelling alone on a road in search of a prized jewel. There are thorns conspicuously planted on that road. Now if you got hurt from stepping on these thorns, would you stop going? Would you choose to turn back home?

Would you study the placement of these thorns and find your way around them, so you could get to your destination? Your answer is not only a test of your decision-making prowess, but also a test of your mental strength. Note that the pain incurred is not mental but physical. Yet the key determinant factor in your decision making is how resilient you are mentally.

The foremost reasons mental toughness is essential is because, as I have come to believe, none of us would live without having any record of failure at one time or another. Since these failures are part of our existence, we must outsmart failure as much as possible. One thing helps you overcome the failure of the past: the fact that you have tried again. This is crucial. We have hundreds of men and women who have attempted certain things at first and failed. Tried again and failed over and over. But the glamour of failure is that it teaches you to be more clinical with your attempt. Today, we are enjoying the results of these FAILURES. Understand me. The reason people are considered successful is because there is such a thing as failure. So, in essence, if there is no failure, we can't have any idea of success. The one thing that differentiates people who tried once, failed and backed out from those who keep trying until they get it right is traceable to how mentally tough they are.

Mental toughness also helps you assess your experiences and learn from them. When we say 'experiences', in most cases, we refer to those things you could have done better or those situations you could have handled in a better way. In essence, we could surmise that experiences in this context are mistakes. Apart from the fact that mental toughness makes you want to try again at those things you've previously failed, you will also get to evaluate yourself and spot the origin of your failure. Once you do this, you will be able to build upon that and correct the mistake. Let's take another example of a lady whose relationship just hit rock bottom all of a sudden, and she's got a lot of problems to deal with. Now if she manages to get out of that pit and find solid ground again, what would be her disposition to love? Would she give someone else a chance to show love to her? Would she hate the idea of love? Her choice would then tell us if she is strong or weak mentally.

Although people might argue that such lady is simply 'guarding her heart', I have very bad news for those who reason like that. The summary of it all is this: playing it safe is for the average who enjoy and intend on living only average lives.

What else does being mentally tough do? Mental toughness makes you become more logical than emotional. For someone who is in the business arena, logic is a stronger tool for decision making than emotions. After recording several crashes in investments and marketing, you become a lot wiser and better with handling things. So, imagine two groups bring their proposals to you as an investor. Consider that the first group has a solid laid out blueprint with measured risks and precautionary measures already outlined, while the second group appears with a less concrete plan but with quite an impressive persuasive speech. Where would you invest your hard-earned money? Now, if you're someone who has had a series of failed investments, you would not discard the concrete for the emotional simply because you have lost before and you don't want to lose again. Mental toughness helps you discard what might not be really beneficial to the interest of you or your company even when persuaded to do so.

Mental strength also helps you to build more confidence in yourself. Your mind is the battlefield where every transaction is done before your body can respond to it. Now only two sides are warring within you, since every moment in life is spent making decisions. Should I do it or not? Should I go or stay? Should I tell her or not? I assume the two sides in conflict in our mind are the positive force and the negative force. The positive force helps to make decisions, while the negative force delays decision making. Mental toughness is what conquers the army of self-doubt in favor of self-confidence. Self-doubt is the greatest embargo on destiny. Mental toughness helps you remove that and opens new door of opportunities.

Mental toughness gives you the courage to discard unhelpful advice no matter where it may emanate from. The mentally weak person might be left with no other choice than other people's choices when the time comes for decision making. Because people who have a weak mentality are always controlled by the spirit of fear. Fear is the 'self-doubt' that I mentioned earlier.

Once you cannot make decisions independently, your business is not likely to thrive as much as you would like.

Mental resilience also helps to reveal the special abilities in you that you might be unaware of. Professional athletes are a great example of this. While I admit that these players are 'naturally gifted', I also believe that, behind the one great free throw in a basketball game, there is an uncomfortable number of failed ones in training. These players might not know of this great talent until after a few failed attempts. What if they had stopped trying after the first attempt that went rocking against the wall? How would they know that they can be grandmasters at that if they gave up after a few unsuccessful trials? Likewise, in every human endeavor, we might not be able to tap into that God-given talent or special ability if we stopped after a few fails.

Finally, mental toughness makes you see the positive side of your situation and circumstances. Believe me, there are some terrible places life can drag you into, and I have had my share of that as well. But it takes only enough mental strength to be able to conquer these battles of life. No matter how hard things may be, mental toughness makes you see the bright side of it. They say that some see roses in thorns and others see thorns in roses. I think that should be self-explanatory as to the two groups of people we have discussed. Positive people have a higher tendency of success than negative people. And without mental strength, you might never attain that level of maximum optimism. My advice for you in that regard is that you should stay positive no matter the situation.

This book is not just meant to TELL you what mental resilience means. It is my belief that, as you read through, I'll be able to SHOW you how to become mentally strong. This has the potential to change you relationships, finances, career and life in general in a way most don't even dare to dream.

Chapter II
Building Mental Toughness

Think of the most beautiful skyscrapers and large structures such as the Eiffel tower. You've really got to think of mental toughness in the perspective of a builder. As big as those buildings are, they are built with the smallest of materials. Stone on a stone, metal on a metal and glass on glass. Well, your existence on earth also follows the same pattern. Nothing is ever achieved without a qualifying process. This simply means you have to build your life to the desired heights. The big news is: you'll never finish building your mentality. It's a Continuum, a process you go through day after day.

The process to build mental strength and toughness is not the same as building physical strength. To grow your body, you need food, water, exercise and other things. On the mental scale, however, the requirements are different. It shouldn't surprise you to know that many people are physically fully developed, yet they possess very little mental strength. We also have some who are younger who are very mentally resilient.

The keyword I am focusing on in this chapter is 'building'. Parallel to the conventional or literal understanding of what it means to build, which is the architectural meaning of it, building in this sense is much more a process that goes on in your mind. So, what are the materials to build with? Experience.

I have said earlier on that experience is vital. Experience can come in two ways. It can be gotten firsthand, that is through your own ordeals and what you've understood by doing, hearing, smelling, seeing, tasting, feeling . . . These I classified as first class because they are your 'property'. The second type is the secondhand experience. These are experiences of other persons you've come to know about. For example, Walt Disney's or Albert Einstein's experiences are secondhand types of experiences to me. While secondhand experiences are good, even great, firsthand experiences are better. This is why science classes are better when practicals are involved. Theories are other people's experiences, while your own experience is the practical. The practicals don't make the theories untrue; they only make them more concrete.

The availability of building materials does not make everybody a builder. Unless you have been trained to be a builder, you might not be able to use your available materials. How then is mental toughness built? How do I add new layers to what is already on ground?

1. Make a balance between your emotions and logic — If we remove emotions from our lives in favor of logic alone, we have caused a big problem. Emotion is the driver of faith. Faith is the handler of risk taking, and taking risk is an essence of living and making massive moves. I believe emotion is one of the things that make us human. Yet I believe we shouldn't be overtly emotional and not have any room for logical reasoning. It's like a pH scale. It must be balanced. I agree that logic is like a firewall preventing loses, hurts, and pain. But what if the logic is wrong? You should be in touch with your emotions without being paranoid. There is always time for everything. You should know which side of yourself to reveal in every situation.

2. Remove negative influences — There are people in your life whose only contribution to your life is to help destroy you, little by little. These are the people who point out the negative part of that step you want to take without considering what is positive about it. They are the very channels that feed your addiction, depression . . . You need to cut off those channels of negativity from your life as soon as possible if you want to become mentally stronger. I have discovered that most of these

people are those you classify as 'indispensable'. Truly, the only one person you can't do without is yourself. This does not mean you should set yourself in solitary confinement forever. You should never forget that you need people around you in order to succeed, but you do not need toxic people who would contaminate and weaken you mentally.

3. Give room for change — For the record I am a creationist. However, Darwin aptly said those who survive the harsh winds of the world are not really the strongest but the ones who can quickly adapt to their environment and situations. The 'strongest' here refer to those with obvious physical advantages. Physical strength is good, but mental resilience is essential for our survival. Adapting to changes or evolving with time is a process that can make you mentally stronger. There are some things you hold on to that you really have to let go to become a better person and a more efficient human. Imagine that, in this digital world of science and technology, someone still walks nine miles to deliver a letter instead of getting in a vehicle simply because he is afraid of getting into a car accident? Or someone who still uses a typewriter when there is a

laptop at his disposal? Embracing the changes that affect that process you've been accustomed to helps to make you mentally tough. Old must give way to the new, if the new is better, but how can you become better when you refuse to change?

4. Don't cover up your weakness — Your weakness is your weakness, not anybody else's. In my observation, I feel that one thing you shouldn't hide from is your weakness. If your weakness is alcohol, every time you deny yourself a beverage you take your mental resilience up just a notch. Some of you, your weakness may be sleep. You say it isn't true, but your actions say you want sleep more than you want success. Every time you set your alarm clock and you slap that weakness in the face you gain just a little more mental resilience. These are small building blocks that turn you into a mental ninja. On second thought, you could turn your weakness into your strength — your selling point. Really, we've had many cases where people turn a disadvantage to an advantage by simply thinking over it. My weakness is patience. Don't mistake what I'm saying... It is for sure a weakness. However, my lack of

patience often drives me even harder when trying to accomplish a task on a timeline.

5. Find time to be quiet — Okay, I know this might sound strange to some of you, but to be factual, everyone needs to meditate and find time to just be quiet. Meditation is a great tool for better understanding of yourself and better understanding of your immediate environment. I am not refereeing to anything super religious or mystical here. Matter of fact have you ever been driving in a quiet car by yourself with no radio on next thing you know you're at your destination you hardly remember the drive at all. Or maybe you were taking a hot shower super relaxed you lose track of time and next thing you know your significant other is banging on the door for you to get out. I would suggest that these are both some form of meditation. You let your thoughts quiet themselves and take a rare moment of quietness. I have two suggestions in regards to what you should add to your morning routine. First, wake up early, sit up, and meditate for some time before engaging in any activity. Meditation helps to boost the efficiency of your brain function and boosts your mental energy. You could dedicate 30 minutes of your

early hours to read your Bible and meditate on it or simply sit and be quiet, for some this may come natural for others It is absolutely excruciating. The second suggestion I will give you is that you should get physical. Exercise is a great stress relief. Getting some form of physical exercise in the morning will sharpen your mind for the day and help you focus. This isn't easy and requires you to exercise a lot of discipline. This results in a compound effect of growing both your mental and physical resilience.

6. Get adequate sleep and find time to relax — Adequate sleep for you might be six hours, seven hours or even eight hours. This depends on how you model your daily activities. Once your body is accustomed to a specific number of hours of daily sleep, don't deny it. Sleep is needed to remain functional with maximum productivity. You also need to give your body some moments of relaxation and enjoyment. Its not all about mental boot camp If you deny your body these two things, your mind won't be at its strongest and healthiest. Like I mentioned earlier, keep in mind, there will be a lot of people who could have succeeded but won't because of one simple thing... Sleep. Although

getting good sleep is important you need to adapt when things need to get done. I add that for those who will read this and twist what I'm trying to say. Be responsible with your sleep but if you haven't earned your 8 hours of sleep don't be a punk and cash in on what you haven't earned that day.

7. Be ready to live with your actions and inactions — Like it or not, there is almost no contribution of 'fate' in how our lives turn out. In fact, I've seen that most of the things we think are 'fate' are the consequences of our activities or the activities of others. As a person who is conscious of the fact that, one way or another, your actions influence your life positively or otherwise, you should be able to make decisions that you can live with. This helps make you mentally stronger, as self-will and confidence come from identifying the results of your actions before doing them. It makes you have an edge over those who are oblivious of what their actions might bring to them... If that is taken into consideration, you will not only get mentally stronger and alert, but you'd also become more responsible.

8. Become less rigid and more flexible — For your mental development, rigidity is a negative thing. Everyone would love to work with a flexible mind, rather than a rigid one — even you! Flexibility means you are easy to please. You don't take things personal when they don't work the way you want them to work. It means that you are ready to reach out halfway and meet those extra requirements even when it puts you at odds with your ideals. So, what do you do when your principles clash with another person's? It doesn't have to throw you off the right path; a mentally strong person would make extra efforts at making things better for both sides. Making that extra attempt builds up your mental strength and your bank account.

9. Validate yourself — Perhaps this is one of the keystones holding your mental toughness intact. You should honestly sit down and ask yourself what your definition of fulfilment is. What does it mean to be rich, comfortable, great, tough, failed, powerful, stupid, phenomenal... Do you need to use another person's life goals as a yardstick to measure your value? What serves as the benchmark for the success you've imagined? While the definitions, answers and

validation of other people might be great, self-validation can never be matched. For you to become tough mentally, you must go by your own standard and at your own pace. You must always be the judge of your own products. 'Good enough' should be decided by you. 'Perfect' should also be your decision. Do not let other people tell you what is good and what is bad. Model your life to your own taste. Your ability to assess yourself and deliver great judgements is just another testimony to the fact that your mental capacity and strength are being boosted.

10. Resist peer pressure — One of the major things that contributes to a weak mentality is peer pressure. Many people do things without considering if it's right for them at the moment. They just think it's cool, or worse, acceptable when they see others doing it. They are just another sheep in a world of sheep living average, luke-warm, sheep life. A fundamental step to boost your mental strength is to decide for yourself whether something is right for you at that moment, regardless of whatever your peers say or do. All your friends/family are getting a college education. Taking jobs in the corporate world with great benefits. Thats great,

nothing wrong it. However, is that what you want? Don't sell out because what you want isn't the acceptable or norm. Can you manage living a life of responsibility and entitlement yet? You have to decide what's best for you, even if your friends are against it.

11. Avoid stereotypes — I strongly believe that one of the most dangerous things along your way to being mentally tough and independent is stereotyping. It's dangerous to your mental sanity. It's more dangerous to your relationships. It can damage your dreams. There are two sides to this stereotyping that I want you to consider. The first one is fitting into a stereotypical box. You can never grow in leap and bounds if you are confined in a box. Once you have accepted a wrong label and you do nothing to fight if off and remove that label, you might never reach your dreams. The second part is when you also carry stereotypical ideas about people, places or things. That also won't help your mental state. Whatever values you will hold, find them out yourself. If it is believed 'those guys can't be trusted with anything' and you've got nothing to prove that, why not refuse to share that view until evidences comes up? Stereotyping can only do one thing: it will bring

you against those you are meant to work with and damage your reasoning. If anything, stereotypical people are only confessing that they are weak, that they can't think for themselves, and that they inherit ideas that are not quite necessary. So, as one way to build your mental strength, don't allow yourself to be stereotyped and never allow stereotypical thinking to become part of your being. You see this a lot in the blue-collar American family when it comes to their ideas and thoughts of the wealthy. You may have had the same thoughts yourself: "They are where they are because they are greedy, selfish, backstabbing" whatever it may be. By having this stereotypical thought, you are literally self-destructing your chances of being wealthy yourself. Why you ask.... Let me explain, if you absolutely HATE I mean despise something do you not do your best to avoid it? This happens subconsciously without you even realizing it. Same goes with money, if every time you see someone with money you place them in a stereotypical box of greed, and selfishness you will certainly subconsciously make decisions to ensure you DO NOT become like them... WEALTHY.

12. Do away with distractions — One last attribute of people who are mentally tough that I will discuss with you in this chapter is that they set their minds on things and get them done without getting distracted. Nobody can get anything done at a specified time if he or she pays attention to distractions. In life, many things can distract us. TV, social media, unexpected visitors, gossips, and most importantly, the almighty cell phone! These things are what you could call time wasters if not used properly. Most of the time, distractions don't discourage you from doing what you want to do; they only make it take longer to complete. So you should find a way to deal with distractions. Anything that could distract you should be as far away from you as possible. This could be as petit as putting the phone on silent or as serious as cutting someone out of your life. You only have one life to live. Don't allow it to be ruled and stifled by b.s distractions. You must live with the consciousness of the transient nature of time. Beat the deadlines. Make it work by removing your distractions.

CHAPTER III
MENTALLY STRONG ENOUGH TO ACHIEVE YOUR DREAMS

Having discussed earlier the meaning of mental toughness, I feel it is appropriate to explain the concept of 'dream'. A dream is a set goal — a proposed target. A dream is a place where the first step is aimed at stopping. It is that particular objective to be achieved by individuals. Dreams are the most necessary ingredient of success recipes. A man who has no dreams has no targets and has no movements. There are, however, two types of dreams/goals. There is a short-term dream/goal and the long-term dream/goal. As their names suggest, a short-term goal is an achievement that one aims at making over a short period of time. The long-term goal, on the other hand, is the bigger picture, the desired end product of one's actions. We could say the long-term goal is the totality of many short-term goals. For an entrepreneur, for example, a short-term goal might be to sell a certain amount of a product for a day, while a long-term goal might be to become a producer of that same product. While short-term goals might be of utmost importance for the time being, the strings of a business are pulled by long-term goals.

I have often asked, both as a young boy and as a man, what are things that make some people more successful than the others? Face value suggest talent. Most of the time (until I find out the truth for myself), I have heard the lie that talented people are more likely to be successful than others. Truth of the matter is that, talent is a raw material. Talent is not a final product. You may never become more successful than others simply because you have the talent. Talent can never sustain you.

I absolutely DESPISE when someone uses the term "Overnight Success." It is an abstraction and simply does not exist. I don't care if it's business, entertainment, sports, or anything for that matter. People fail to see the countless failures, sleepless nights, and constant hustle it takes to "make it." Many do not know what you have gone through in your closet or the rejections you have endured. Many simply chose to ignore the fact that you have tried countless times before hitting that target. That is why I love the quote by Leo Messi which says: "I start early and stay late. Day after day, year after year. It took me 17 years and 114 days to become an overnight success." Did you hear that? 17 whole years of little by little yet consistent progress. If I may ask; is that what an overnight success really means? If it is, then I have no problem with the terminology. But if an 'overnight success' is someone who started a business in a day and made a million dollars or someone who hits sudden jackpots at the casino on the first try... If that is an overnight success, then I do not think any such thing exists. You must put in the work and be willing to take the blows! Life is not magic. I have heard this myself at times: "Man, N-Tact really blew up for ya overnight." Or "Must be nice owning your own business and making your own hours." These people were sleeping when I was working 7P to 7A two hours away from home. Asleep by 930AM and back up to do it again that night. They didn't see me when I was driving for Uber and Lyft all night and then dragging my butt into my office the next day. Owning something great and becoming something great requires a great deal of mental and physical sacrifices. Anyone who wants to achieve anything great must make great sacrifices to achieve it. It is such a simple law of living. In the words of Grant Cardone: "Success is your frickin' responsibility." You need to own it, and it takes responsibility for your life. No one, and I mean NO ONE, truly cares if you make it like you do.

Someone recently contacted me on Instagram (@Mitchellrtucker). They wanted to know if I could provide them with any tips, tricks, or ideas on how to obtain an investor for a business idea he had. He told me he had an investor in mind, but that he wasn't giving him the time of day and wanted to know if I had any ideas on how he could get his attention. He explained to me his business plan, and it sounds pretty solid. There is risk in everything, especially in the business world, but it was reduced risk for sure. (Have it at the back of your mind that it takes a lot of risk-taking to survive in this world.) I asked him how much money he needed, and it was roughly 75K dollars. He wasn't asking for that much and was willing to give 50% of the business. The business plan seemed solid, and he had a positive track record, so I was curious at this point as to why he was having such difficulty obtaining an investor. I asked him, how much money have you put in, and he said: "Well, I haven't put any money in really, just my time." So you only need 75K and you want the investor to put up all the money? He tells me yes... I click on his IG profile, and every other picture on IG is him standing next to a beautiful Mercedes. I don't recall what model, but it was a newer model, so it is irrelevant. I asked him, is that your Mercedes in all those pictures, and he told me that it was. I told him that is a beautiful car and asked how much he paid for it. As he swelled with pride, I'm sure, he tells me that he just purchased it and that he paid 65K for it. My response to him. Sir, I don't mean to be rude, but I would not give you a penny. I would never give anything to anyone to help them make their dreams come true, if they are not willing to sacrifice for them also. I told him, if he is serious about wanting to make this happen, he needs to sell his Mercedes and re-approach his investor. Joint business opportunities are one thing, but when you are seeking full financial backing because you cannot do it yourself, please don't pull up in a Mercedes.

A lot of you really want to make it. You want to travel around the world and show up at the beach with a full tan and the most expensive wines in hand. You have these crazy dreams and business ideas you want to start, but frankly, you don't deserve them. You don't deserve them because you have a Mercedes in your life and you're not willing to sacrifice the comfort and luxury it provides towards a greater course. It may not be a beautiful 65K dollar car; it may be an obsession with trending clothes, tech, nights out with the guys or girls. Maybe it's where you live, maybe you need to give up that beautiful apartment and downscale for a while. Reduce your data plan and stay on Wi-Fi. It sounds ridiculous, but without realistic sacrifice and hard work, you don't deserve to "make it".

Life isn't easy, and you may discover that the second you get a few thousands saved up and start feeling good about yourself, you get hit with some more nonsense. If you stay in your rut and accept the idea that you are defeated and broken, you will remain defeated and broken.

When surveys are done, it is said that almost all marriage issues are caused due to financial stress. Financial stress can become a chronic issue and being mentally tough to get through the hard times is often all that is needed before seeing the light at the end of the tunnel. You can read 100 books on setting the right mindset, and if you're not smart with your money, you will get drained quickly! Bottom line is you need to change your mindset and get your approach to money right before anything else!

The mindset of having "just enough." Or "be happy with what you have." "Be thankful you were born in America." "There are a lot of others less fortunate than you." All of these cliché crappy comments are very true. However, the most selfish thing you can do is remain where you are. Ok, you're content you have everything you need, right? What about the person lying in the hospital bed unsure how they are going to afford the treatments they so desperately need? Are you in a position to help that person? Ok, you live in America, congrats. But I'm sure most people reading this book do... We all know that America is a great nation. But America isn't Utopia. America doesn't have everything for everyone. There are many Americans who are in need of basic necessities: food, clothing, good housing... Are you in a position to provide jobs for other

Americans who are looking to put food on the table for their family? There are a lot of people who are less fortunate than you are. Absofrickianlutely right, that's why you need to get your money right, so you can make a difference in others' lives. You see, that ideology — of being content and 'thankful to God' even for your 'just enough' budget that is so engraved in a lot of us is quite harmful, and it couldn't be further from the truth.

Everything God ever created strives to be its best. A tree doesn't sprout from a seed thinking it's tired and only going to grow half of its ability. It grows as tall as it possibly can with what resources it has.

A lion, when chasing its prey, does not run at half speed. It makes the decision and then goes all in. Why do we, as humans, made in the image of God himself, choose to go through life half throttle? Why do we not thrive to reach our full potential like everything else on earth? Why do we lift up our eyes and declare a task 'impossible'?

We have been told our whole lives that we should get a job, make an honest living, support our family, and if we have just a little excess, that's ok, but we shouldn't strive for more than that. When we change our mindset, I can guarantee you, making the money you want and having the life you dreamed of is a lot more obtainable than you ever thought. Believe me, there is no sin in having more than you need (if you earned it the right way, of course). If you could simply change the mindset of partially fulfilled lifestyle, you would discover, much to your amazement, that life is much more fun than it used to be.

A side note here: I have come across so many people that claim to have the mindset of an entrepreneur. They say all the right things because they have watched enough Gary V or Grant Cardone videos, but when it comes to taking action, they are lifeless. Not everyone can do what you do. As soon as I started to "make it" (I use that term loosely ;)) the first thing I wanted to do is bring people on board with me. You have to ask yourslef the tough questions: how will this improve my business ventures? How can others benefit from this? How do I carry on this plan smoothly without affecting others negatively?

I had a brand-new mindset, and things were panning out. I saw a whole new way of operating, and I wanted others to "see the light" as well. Truth is I believe everyone has it in them, but not everyone will do it. If you don't have a WHY that makes you cry at night, you're not hungry enough for success. If you aren't mentally tough, you're not ready for this.

While chasing your dreams, life will chew you up and spit you out more times than the average person can handle. I contacted Deputies I had worked with and friends to tell them about opportunities. Half of them smirked, and the other half jumped on board for 30 days and died out. Once you're in the position, you can't wrap your mind around why people don't want more. It is not laziness most of the time; a lot of these people are incredibly hard workers. It always comes down to mindset and being as tough mentally as they are physically. One always complements the other. You would discover that many people are not as hardworking as others you have seen, yet they are making it big time even more than those who work harder. The answer to it is that, while the former type of people complements their mental strength with physical strength, the other group of people might not have the sufficient mental energy to drive through the seemingly knotty parts of the process. Don't be surprised that physical strength doesn't automatically result in success. Where physical efforts may fail, one who will be successful must have a great deal of mental strength to try again.

Before we move on, let me share with you the formula I have employed over time.

Correct mindset + Helping others + Grit = Success

Think of everyone who has an abundance of wealth. What is something they all have in common? If thoughts of greed and evil come to mind, start from the beginning of this chapter and re-read until you're ready to move on to something a little deeper. The answer is quite simple — They all solve problems in some way or another. Maybe it is in the health sector, entertainment, safety, business, convenience, and in every other niche of human engagements. They see a need in the market, and they fill that gap. This is what it is all about. Correct your mindset, find the need, and grind to make it happen. There are many examples of men and women who have done this that we can look to: Mark Zuckerberg is a billionaire today because he was able to solve the problem of communication to a large and reasonable extent. Uber is thriving today because the company identified an essential need of people, and they are able to leverage on that to bring about their ideas, which are now full blown today. Identifying people's needs is the first step to becoming that great man or woman you have dreamt of becoming. Now, I must say these societal needs might be new, or you have discovered that those needs have not been adequately met by others. Taking Uber as an example, once again, we realize this company didn't build vehicles for transportation. They only modified an already provided solution to fit their plan. You must also try to bank on a situation or desperate need of your society or community to have your big break. So, simply put, the people who are enjoying wealth today fall into a small circle of solution providers. Keep that in mind.

I had 10 years of law enforcement experience. I started in law enforcement as a Deputy Sheriff at the age of 19 years old. I turned in my badge and gun on December 20th, 2017 and decided to start my own business. I come from a family of entrepreneurs, and I guess you can say it was in my blood.

I always had this dream of owning my own business and achieving the financial freedom people dream about. I could not do either while being a cop and certainly not without a plan. I developed my plan, and I turned in my badge. The comments I received from my friends and coworkers were less than encouraging. People don't like change; average people don't quit careers and take risk. When you do things that are outside the norm of "average," it makes people feel uncomfortable. On top of that, as sad as it is, people typically don't want to see you succeed. So if you always think that all those who flash their smiles at you or those who give you their 'honest advice" actually wish you good, you're on a very long road. Many times, we get laid back by ourselves because we just can't wrap our heads around the thoughts of beginning again on a different and new system. Then we might begin reconsidering staying put in our profession. Then, slowly and silently through the back door, our limiting mindset crawls in again until our dreams either get postponed or even totally sidelined. I could have been retired with a great pension at 45. I get it, but that wasn't my dream.

The reality is this: although you might have prepared well for what your future will look like and what your next line of action will be, there are always some unforeseen circumstances or even oversights. So don't be disillusioned into thinking that when you have simply made the right decisions, everything else will fall into place. In my case, what I was not prepared for mentally was the financial stress that came along with quitting a career and chasing my dream. Yes, this was self-induced. I wasn't laid off, and I didn't come down with an illness that left me unable to work. However, I went through it, so I'm hoping

I can share with you my experience and how you can get through it likewise.

It is true cops do not make a lot of money, not nearly what they should in my opinion; however, I assure you it is a lot more than nothing :).

I was fortunate enough to start collecting a check and making some money immediately, but it took mental toughness and determination to grow that check and push through the hard times. I was 29 years old, and my blood pressure was running 155/99! I was not prepared mentally to handle what I put my family and myself into, and a lot of lessons were learned along the way.

If you have ever made a cold call, you know just how detrimental it can be to your very soul after being cussed at and hung up on 100 times a day. This was my new reality, and I loved it! You must, once again, set your Why. You will see this a lot throughout this book, with the common theme in the realm of being mentally tough. If you don't have a why, you will fail every time. If your stress is self-induced like mine was and you do not have a strong why, then why put yourself through this hell? Go back to your JOB, get your guaranteed check, and live your whole life with only moderate stress but know that you will only live moderately like this! You will never reach your full potential and impact the world like you could have. Most reading this chapter aren't looking to live an average life, so mentally prepare yourself now to take the blows. You must truly take risks, but do not just take risks; take calculated risks! Nothing great has ever been done without some form of risk. This is true in everything we do. Falling in love, getting pregnant, heck, a trip to your local Walmart. You know you are taking a risk once you begin asking yourself the "what ifs". Calculated risks mean you go ahead and ask yourself further questions while simultaneously providing answers that will serve as your "game plan". "When this happens, what will be my next step?" "How will I recover my capital if this plan does not work?". . . Everything requires some form of risk, and typically, the higher the risk, the bigger the payout. What we need to do is make good decisions and calculated risk. Risk without research is reckless, but calculated risk is how millionaires are made. Let me share with you the top five things I wish I was more familiar with before I started this adventure. These are the 5 things I did in order to stay mentally tough during these hard-financial times.

1.) Believe things will improve. If you have made it this far, you probably have already grasped the idea that staying positive is one of the most important things you can do. I don't care if you don't really believe it. You need to lie to yourself and do it daily! Yes, I am telling you to lie... DAILY!.. Funny thing about pathological liars, they lie so much and so often that they truly start to believe what they are saying is the truth. They turn their lie into their reality, and although I don't condone lying to other people for gain, you need to lie to yourself daily for gain! It is an integral part of what helps you form a formidable mentality. If you want, you could call it 'self-motivation'. Tell yourself those things that aren't so much in full view and address them as though they are already in your grasp. Believe it, and you can conceive it. Problems = Progress.. Solve enough of them and you will reach your goal.

2.) Widen your circle, know who you can trust and who you get ideas from. Although it is true that every human has different personalities and attitudes, yet for a person who aims at building a successful business, it is paramount to widen your circle. It may be just as important to shrink your circle! Most have heard statements like: "You are the sum of the 5 people you hang out with the most," or "Birds of a feather flock together." There are hundreds of little phrases that all basically mean the same thing. I think it would be wise, for the purpose of clarity, that widening your circle should be in two stages. First, at the formative stage of your business idea, when you identify the societal need, it is advisable to get to know those needs better. Who is it meant to help? How would they prefer it? How have others tried to do it before? You can't get every answer to those questions in your closet alone. You need to get outside and get firsthand information from those who need your solution. Second, every entrepreneur needs to move with like minds who will not only help you in building your own ideas and business because of their varying insights, but who will also spur you to action in the process. Bottom line is this: if you want to be rich, hang out with rich people. If you want to get into shape, hang out with people who are in better shape than you are. Like minds sharpen each other (or weaken each other, depending on which group you fall into). As easy as this sounds, it can be just as detrimental for you if you don't do it. Hang out with people who eat horrible and you will eat horrible; hang out with poor people, and you will feel comfortable being poor. You must widen your circle, reach out to people that are more advanced than you in the areas you want to succeed in. Not only will you make great connections, such as investors, mentors, and business leaders, but it will motivate you to be and do more with your life. This is not necessarily a how to book, but I want to tell you briefly how to do this, because I heard this statement: "Widen your circle," a hundred times before I figured out just how to do it. It's easy to say, but how do you do it!?

First, you must force yourself to be a little extrovert. "Well that's just not me, Mitchell. I can't do that." Ok, stay poor, man! I don't know what to tell you, but you're going to be uncomfortable. Yes, it sucks... Anyways.... Social media is your friend. Find local people in your area of work or in the area of work you want to be in that are killing it. If you are a car sales man and you want to be the best car sales man, find out who the best is. Connect with them in person or on social media. ALWAYS, ALWAYS approach with a compliment first! No one would appreciate someone showing up for the first time in their Facebook inboxes and begin an awkward chat right away. Not even a competitor in a perfect market!

Never ask them right off the rip for advice, a favor or anything. It goes like this: "Bob, hey I see we are in the same market. I just wanted to reach out to you and let you know I really respect what you're doing. I hear great things and see that you're killing it! Maybe we can do lunch sometime. I would love to pick your brain. Do you have lunch plans for Thursday?" Identify right away why you're messaging them, compliment them, tell them what you want, and pick a day. Never leave it open. Pick an upcoming day and make it within a week. In that way, you have successfully put them in a tight position where it would be seemingly impossible for them to turn you down. They will be more likely to meet with you, and if they truly can't due to scheduling conflicts, they will feel obligated to pick a date and schedule it right then and there.

This topic really deserves a whole book on its own, but the above information is one of the most powerful techniques you can use. Try it out and let me know how it works for you!

3.) Make A Plan — Come up with a plan and stick with it. I truly believe God helps those who help themselves or at least tries to! Step one does you NO good if you are sitting around waiting for something to fall into your lap.

You are not wealthy, because honestly, you don't deserve to be at this point in your life! You don't deserve it because you've not done the right things long enough. Don't think that because you've suffered at some point you thereafter deserve to become a sudden billionaire. And if you've gotten this far in this book and resolved to follow the step by step guide this book provides, then I can say you're on the right track and only need to stay focused on the road ahead. Now you have to decide HOW you're going to get to your goals and then stick with it. Don't chase every shiny object or every grand idea that comes to mind.   I'm guilty of this more than most.

I get easily excited when I see potential in something and want to chase and do everything. Stay motivated and eager to work but stay smart and focused. Once you have your plan in place, write it down... and then.... Write it down again. Your plan essentially becomes your to do list, which becomes your goals, which would later become your list of accomplishments! Just so you know, you might have many great and exciting ideas in your head, but you might find it really difficult to put everything in place. You might be able to integrate two, three, four, or even more ideas into a unified whole, even when those ideas and plans are independently laid out, but the fact remains that you can't do everything altogether.

4.) Take action. There is a thing about ideas; without action they are dead. Or worse still, those ideas are worked upon by someone else. And you know, life is a messed-up place. You'd later find out that it could have been your experience and gains, and you'd either weep in your closet or play second fiddle to someone else. Take action and take it fast! DO NOT wait until you have everything down perfect; you never will. I once heard imperfect action results in imperfect results; however, imperfections can be improved upon. On the contrary, no action results in no results. Clearly, I would rather have imperfect results than no results.

Don't let your dreams slip away because you were too scared or too lazy to put in the work. Take time to establish a plan and then attack it with everything you have like a charging rhino. The word "decision" is powerful. You should always take your time when making decisions, but when you make a decision, it should be final! There should be no other options than what you decide. Decisions are the spark that ignites massive explosion in change. Progress isn't magical. Progress is simply the result of good decisions.

5.) Invest in yourself: There is one important fact I would like you to understand. Never forget it: You are your greatest asset your business venture has. Not that huge capital you have in bank or the checks you've received from your customers. What happens to your business when you, as the organizer, are not available, especially for someone whose idea just got kick-started? You must invest in yourself, being the greatest asset of your enterprise, to become not only better but also more efficient. Whatever financial situation you may be facing at this point, you can always find a way to invest in yourself. Read books, take classes, watch videos. Join a local library, attend conferences. . . I encourage you to read every book you can in your industry. Not everyone enjoys reading, but someone who wants to build a successful business must be a reader. If initially not to 'enjoy' the read, but most importantly to draw out useful advice.

I personally hated reading. I am getting much better, but it's a struggle for me. I love audiobooks though. Look up the books in your industry that are making waves and look for them in audio format if you can't sit down and read them. You want to be a beast; well, I am telling you the secret of the beast! This is not only applicable to your industry but every other industry. Task yourself. Give yourself targets, penalize yourself when you do not meet them, because you are the only recognized umpire in your business. Successful people invest in themselves. They read, take classes, and watch videos. They make a conscious decision to be the best and whoever invests in themselves the most becomes the best, not only mentally but physically. I cannot stress enough how important it is for you to work on your physically health also. Feeling healthy does more for your mental health than you could ever imagine. Invest the time necessary to ensure you are taking care of you!

I was lucky as a kid my parents put me into Martial arts which I feel changed me as an adult in so many ways. I started Martial arts when I was roughly 12 years old and instantly fell in love with it. I was blessed to have found one of the very few (in my opinion) legitimate schools! We trained the way it was supposed to be. Concrete floors, no A/C, no plush mats and participation trophies. My instructor was an Olympic medalist, military veteran and just an all-around bad dude when it came to the arts he studied and taught. I remember one day I was the only student that showed up for Hapkido (the art I study.) This was common during those times when we were training in that particular building. I was a few years in, and I was somewhere in the ballpark of 14-15 years old.

We started the class in our normal fashion, and he tells me, ok were going to do a conditioning day, I knew when he said that it was going to be absolute hell! We started with some quick push-ups, sit-ups and the typical exercises and then we moved to the bag. He set his timer and told me to start throwing combinations on the bag. I kicked and punched for what felt like a lifetime. The second I would slow up or drop my arms he would yell and add a minute to my time. FINALLY, I heard the buzzer my arms drop, and I felt the incredible feeling of freedom for just one second. He yelled at me: "Mitchell, lets go!" as he ran out of the building. I chased after and we ran for once again what felt like forever. Me personally, I have never been much of a runner, always hated it and I often told people that's why I learned martial arts, so I wouldn't have to :).. My instructor on the other hand could run forever without breaking a sweat.

We make it back to the heavy bag and he starts the timer again. Let's go he says, start throwing combos. I started again and suddenly I started to feel a little weird, the bag was moving in ways that it shouldn't and no matter how hard I tried to keep my eyes open it was like they were shutting on me... I think I'm going to... and yes, I fainted.

My instructor grabbed me set me in front of a fan and gave me some water. He said let me know when your good to finish. I sat there for maybe a minute max and he told me ok let's go, get up. I went back to the heavy bag under the impression I had a whole round to go but I didn't say anything I got up and started on the bag again. About 30 seconds in he stopped me and told me to take a seat. He reached into a box and pulled out a black belt uniform. Instantly I recognized what it was. He handed it to me and told me if you take this you have to shake my hand and promise me you will continue to train till you get your black belt.

I took the uniform and made the commitment to him. A decision that I benefit from still today. Years later I am a second-degree black belt and operated my own Martial arts school teaching Hapkido at 19 years old.

I never forgot that lesson he taught me. Some may say that's a little ridiculous or maybe a little too rough, I don't know, I would argue that it was exactly what I needed. I didn't even realize what he was doing or that there was a lesson to be learned there until I was much older and had my own school.

I started to see it in my students. If I turned my head and someone stopped doing pushups and started again when I looked their way, I would be willing to bet you, that student wont last. On the other hand, the students who showed up early, stayed late and always did just one more rep or one more round. Those students never quit. My instructor was not testing my physical abilities, he knew where my limits where. My instructor purposely pushed me until I reached my limits not to see how far I could go physically but to test my mental resilience. To see if and when I reach my limit, do I push myself or shut down, to see if I deserved to wear that uniform. As a kid my dream was to one day wear that black belt and more importantly to be able to say I earned it.

As an adult, my goals may have changed direction, but every single kick and every single punch is still very applicable. Are you mentally tough enough to achieve your goals?

CHAPTER IV
MENTALLY TOUGH THROUGH ILLNESS

O ne of the most clichéd sayings that flies around is: tough times never last, but tough people do. Tough times. Tough people. Tough words. Tough meanings. Tough realities. That saying is partially true. (Mind me.) But how many people really grasp the meaning of it, or further still, how many people really live with that in mind as a guiding principle? Of a truth, tough times are tough times. Like humans, some tough times last more than others. What is actually a tough time for anyone? A day or two when you walk around with basically no money? Or a slight headache that's unfamiliar to your body? Come on! Tough times vary, but there is always a common strike through about it: Tough times always shake us to the roots. When your company is suffering from one major financial crisis or the business owner suddenly develops cancer . . . That's the real deal! These are not pleasant happenings, of course, but they are the true "trials of faith". If you're mentally weak, you will be under pressure and the business will collapse. Tough times. Tough people. This chapter discusses the moments of really crazy illness that you can face, either as a business owner or an individual who wants to develop a stronger mentality.

This chapter means a lot to me, as my dad was physically ill my entire life. My dad, Ken Tucker, was diagnosed with

Scleroderma when my mother was pregnant with me in 1988. The doctors gave my father approximately 7 years to live, and he passed away while writing this book in September 2018 just shortly after his 60th birthday.

It still does not seem real to me as I write this. My dad was nothing short of a mental bad @$$, and I gain a large part of my inspiration in writing this book from him. Approximately (3) three years ago, in 2016, I discovered all of these "help groups" and Facebook pages of other Scleroderma "victims." I reached out to a lot of them and wanted to learn more about the illness. I wanted to know what other people were doing, the treatments that were working, and gain some knowledge, so I could help my dad. What I saw repeatedly were these young people that were diagnosed with this horrible illness, and just a few short years later, they had passed away. These people were completely and utterly submersed in researching the latest cures and blogging on their illness. They were the go-to people on anything and everything Scleroderma.

I talked to my dad about getting involved and talking to these people, and he said something to the extent of: I wouldn't even know what to tell them. I don't even know how to spell Scleroderma, son. It's funny, but that one sentence alone holds so much value. When my dad was sick, they ran all kinds of tests. When the results finally came back that it was Scleroderma, the doctor told him what it was, and he asked the doctor if it was contagious. The doctor told him it was not, and the first thing he said was: "Thank God it's Scleroderma." The doctor told him: "Ken, this is a very serious illness, and it needs to be taken seriously." My dad told him: "I don't care how serious it is if it's not contagious." The doctor began to explain the disease to him and the side effects he may begin to experience, and he cut the doctor off. He told the doctor, "If I know what the side effects are, I'm certain to experience them. I don't want to know how to even spell it."

My dad suffered with Scleroderma for 30 years, and up until the day he passed, he never knew a thing about this horrible disease. This is obviously not any form of medical advice, and if you are suffering from an illness, I do suggest getting a professional medical opinion. However, let me tell you what helped my dad. My dad was blessed to have my mother, Bobbi Tucker. She is nothing short of an angel herself, and a mental bad @$$. (She will really hate that I refer to her as that.) My mom did the research and studied up on the best doctors, medicines, and natural cures and made him drink healthy concoctions, experimental natural drugs etc. If it's out there, she researched it and shoved it down his throat. This brings me to my first point, and that is having strong support.

Having a strong support system behind you is vital for your success when dealing with illness. It is not quite the best time to remain reclusive when an illness beckons. Mental toughness, in this case, means that you refuse to give in to that disease. It means you are hell-bent on beating that illness. It is also of enormous importance to have people around you who would help sustain your hope and strength for a longer time. Illness is more of a war, and you need more soldiers to fight along with you. You may not know, but a little smile from someone can improve your immune system. Maybe you are reading this, and you don't have family to support you the way my father had. Get plugged in somewhere. Find a solid church family, join a support group in your city, cling to a best friend, find someone.

This is vital for your success, and regardless of who you are and where you are in life, there are people that care about you. If you are fortunate to have a significant other who is on this journey with you, tell them that you would prefer not to know the symptoms. That you prefer not to mark the calendar in anticipation of death and pain. You will handle them when they come; you only want to know what you need to do to get better. You can do the research yourself, but I strongly suggest not reading anything negative. I've seen people diagnosed with Scleroderma, and the very next day, they are on disability sitting in a rocking chair. They were completely capable of working and functioning the day prior to receiving their diagnosis, but suddenly after receiving the official diagnosis, they are sick. This sends people to their grave so much faster, and it is ALL a mental game. Figure out your why. Ask yourself, what is your why? Why fight, why win, why move forward? If you can't think of a reason why, then you will certainly fail. There is always a why. If you are still on this earth, there is a reason.

Let that be your why in itself. If you have no reason, no why for moving forward, you will only take steps backwards.

Control your thoughts! It's easy for our thoughts to drift into negativity when we are ill. This is even more dangerous when we suffer from terminal illnesses or diseases that the medical world labels "incurable." Your thoughts are so extremely powerful, and if you don't control your thoughts, you will wind up losing yourself. In basketball, they will tell you to watch the player's chest. Your opponent can fake you out with his hands, legs, and head, but he can't go anywhere without his chest. The same goes with your thoughts. Regardless of your circumstances (metaphorically your arms, legs, and head), nothing can go in the direction it needs to go until your thoughts are right first. Determine what outcome you want, engrave it into your mind, and then see it through in your life.

We had a surprise party for my grandma (my fathers' mom) just prior to him passing. What he didn't realize is that the surprise party was for him also. We told my grandma it was for my dad and my dad that is was for grandma:) He went into the hospital on a Thursday. He had a defibrillator in his chest, and that night it went off 30 something times before they could get it under control. He eventually ended up in Shands, where he was shocked a total of 70 something times. In between shocks, he told the doctor: "You need to get this figured out. I have to be out of the hospital by noon on Saturday." The doctor replied: "Well Ken, let's get this figured out first and we'll talk about... Clear.... Shock." My dad had a goal to be out by Saturday, and his mind was so set on it that being shocked at 220 Jewels, whatever that means, couldn't take his mind off his goal! On Saturday at 12 PM, he was released from the hospital and made it to his party! My dad was determined to see his family who was coming from Ohio, and nothing was going to stop him, not even death itself. A few days later, he ended up in the hospital again.

Once again, he told the doctors that he needed to be out in three days because his best friend was coming into town to see him. Against all odds, my dad left the hospital three days later and met his friends at his house where they were able to spend valuable time together prior to him passing. My dad had goals, little milestones that he set in his mind. Things he wanted to accomplish before leaving this world, and once he set those goals, death itself could not keep him from completing them.

When you're sick, often things only get worse before they get better. Make up your mind that you are going to be mentally strong. Do this in the beginning before being mentally strong is your only option. Just like physical strength, you can't join a weightlifting competition and expect to work out the night before and have the desired results the following day. Every result that is being achieved is a direct offspring of actions and efforts behind the scenes. As life is full of uncertainties, one must quickly recognize this and prepare ahead for the different bends in the road. Let me tell you this: Life will throw curve balls at you, and you might not be able to catch them if you don't prepare well enough. The miraculous, the superficial, and the magical are not the ideological pillars that hold businesses in place. It is only fact, action, and resilience that serve as guiding principles. So, in essence, you have to plan ahead for the good and the ugly.

Work on setting goals and getting your mind right before you are put in these situations. My dad never had to second-guess his decisions when he was sick. He knew what he wanted to do and what he wanted to accomplish every step of the way. If you are very ill and mobility is your first goal, engrave it into your mind. Make that a desire so strong that nothing can keep you from accomplishing it. Combine that with your why and make it happen! Motivation is crap. Heck, most people are even wrongly motivated! Don't rely on being motivated every day because that fades with the music, the video, the voicemail, the speech... Your why is the only thing that never fades and only grows stronger. Once that why, that foremost reason of beginning has not been adequately met, then you need to do even more to make it happen. When you are ill, it should be a driving force for you to get through and get back on your feet.

Acceptance is a huge part of getting through your illness. Accept the fact that this is your reality and your life is going to change. Accept the fact that you need people to support you in such critical moments. Accept the fact that, to get out of the uncomfortable position that sickness drove you into, you have to be proactive and follow medical guidelines. Then you must accept the fact that things will surely change. It doesn't always mean that it must change negatively but that it will change. Your morning routine of eating donuts may need to change to a healthier alternative; your binge-watching TV may need to change to one episode and a walk. You may need to reduce your work hours and sleep more. You must do what it takes to move forward and affect change positively; you need to accept that fact and make it happen. Have a talk with your support group, the people you spend the most time with. Let them know that the life you were living before is no longer acceptable due to a new health-wise reality. You have to list the changes that need to be made, whatever they may be. If those people truly love you, they will support and encourage you to make the changes that are necessary for success. They will also help you monitor your progress as well as assist you with things that need to be done.

Listen to medical professionals, but realize they are only human. Most of the time, the advice and insight these people have to offer might be detrimental to your psyche. You still need their instructions. The best thing to do in a case such as this is to safeguard your mental health and follow the prescriptions of the medical personnel. If my dad had taken the words of medical professionals to heart every time they told him the odds were unbeatable, he would have been gone 23 years earlier. Nothing is impossible, and if you have been given an expiration date, just realize that was given to you by another human being, who is full of flaws.

In the words of my father: "There are only two people who are going to tell me when it's my time, and that is me and God." Engrave that into your mind, and if you receive that news, be responsible with your time but also realize you and God are the only ones that can make the decision.

Hold strong to your faith. Faith in the life of anybody is indispensable. Faith as we know it means believing in what might not yet be feasible — what might still be more of an abstraction than a reality. Faith is mixed with optimism and rightly so. We most of the time, faith is regarded as a religious term. Although it is true that faith might have to do with the metaphysical or the spiritual, faith is a much simpler thing. Faith exists in all of us, although in different dimensions. For someone in the business sector of human endeavors, faith is much more concrete. Simply put, faith is the inner assurance that makes risk taking possible. Faith is a high probability. When you are certain that a process will be successful even before trying, then that is faith. Faith therefore is simply OPTIMISM. Of course, the source of our faith differs from person to person. So my advice to anyone who is experiencing a turbulent time right now is this: be optimistic about your illness. Have faith that that situation will be bettered. I am a Christian. I believe I am saved by grace through faith, and that brings so much comfort. I know it did for my father as well. I know there is only one great physician, one physician that can heal all and does not look at medical research and statistics when making decisions. The Bible says, with the faith the size of a mustard seed, you can move mountains. Have faith in Christ and be unstoppable.

Random maybe, but I was at a goat farm this week with my wife and kids. Fun fact we raise goats on our little farm. I say we its mainly my wife but I like to play farmer every now and then :) I saw this goat walking on, I guess what you would consider their knees and I asked the farmer: "Why is that goat walking everywhere on her knees."

The farmer explained to me that when she was very young (8 + years ago) she was diagnosed with a disease called founders (Don't quote me on that spelling) The farmer said she is perfectly fine now, the vet said she should have no pain and there is no sign of any disease left. However, in the goat's mind, she is still very limited. In her mind she can't get off her knees because for over a year she was stuck on her knees. For an entire year she ate, played, walked and ran all on her knees. Now, physically she is very strong and capable. However, her mind limits her physical ability.

Your sick, not dead. Don't allow your mindset to limit you more than your body does. Get off your knees!

CHAPTER V
MENTALLY TOUGH THROUGH FAILURE

It was Thomas J. Watson that said: "Would you like me to give you a formula for success? It is quite simple, really double your rate of failure. You are thinking of failure as the enemy of success but it isn't at all. You can be discouraged by failure or you can learn from it, so go ahead and make mistakes. Make all you can because, remember that is where you will find success."

That is simply a truth many do not want to agree with. You've really got to fail before success can ever come. Collins Powell also said a similar thing: "There is no secret to success; it is the result of preparation, hard work and learning from failure."

When we say failure, what do we mean? Failure is not necessarily a big thing. Failure might be the little unmet targets in your daily progression. The lapsing deadlines, the unbalanced daily sales record, inability to deliver goods to certain customers (even temporarily), these little failures are what contribute to the big failure. So you should take every development seriously. Know this, failures are steppingstones to greatness. If you want to do anything great the only way to get there is to fail your way there. Your reaction to failure is what determines rather or not you deserve success.

No matter how meticulously laid down your plan is, you are bound to fail at some point. If I can assure you of anything, that will be it: you will fail. Not always, but it is sure to happen at some point. Failure is inevitable. Like death, it will visit us all at some point or another. After all, that is always an expected result of risk. Risk will yield either positive results or negative ones. When such risks take a negative result, it is said to have failed. It's not about if you fail — it is how you fail and what you take away from that experience that matters most.

As the legendary Les Brown says: "When life knocks you down, try to land on your back. Because if you can look up, you can get up." Read that again if you need to; it's powerful. That mentality is what you need in order to deal with and remain mentally tough through failure. I have noticed a trend I would like to point out. If you do nothing, you have no chance of failure. If you have failed at something, I want to say: congratulations, welcome to the club. Its members consist of Mr. Steven Spielberg, Thomas Edison, Albert Einstein, Jerry Seinfeld, Abraham Lincoln, Oprah Winfrey, Stephen King, Elvis Presley, Michael Jordan, and the list goes on and on, but I think you get the point.

All these individuals were turned down, told they were uneducated, irrational and/or irrelevant. When you take action, there exists a clear cut between you and the rest of the world. You refuse to sit idle; you refuse to live an average life only to lay in a hospital bed regretting the years you spent living a lukewarm life. I am not here to motivate you; motivation feels good, but it's garbage most of the time. I am here to tell you to stop feeling bad for yourself. The truth is that no one cares about you as much as you do. So what are a few things you can do to help yourself deal with failure on a massive scale? I have a few things listed here that I believe you can use to bounce back from failed ventures.

1.) Acceptance – Accepting the fact that you have failed and moving on as fast as possible. It will definitely hurt when you think of how much you've sacrificed to make it work out to no avail or how much time that could have been channeled into other things that just went down the drain. It will hurt, but it will help you in the long run. Accept when something is a flop, bad idea etc. and figure a new angle of attack. This holds a lot more value than one would initially think. So many people spend years of their lives trying to make a puzzle piece fit. Unless you drop it and pick up a different piece, you're only wasting your time. The theory behind business is like this: When you start a process and along the line make a mistake, the final result wouldn't be what you originally pictured. So you have to accept that as a fact and rework your strategy.

2.) Ask yourself WHY you failed – Realize why you failed. This has two parts, like previously mentioned, the first reason you failed is because you are doing something that no one else is doing (at least not the average person) and as such, there is no prototype to model after. Be proud of yourself that you had the courage to step out and do it.

Now to get more technical, why did it fail precisely? Was this a promotion you have been working on? Or a project that suddenly plummeted from the green zone into nowhere in particular? What made the other person more valuable? Why haven't you received good feedback from your clients? Why has that 'masterplan' suddenly turned out to be total garbage at the end of the day? Well, you know Life isn't always fair. Maybe your competitors aren't more valuable; many times, people just think you suck and don't want to give you the chance.

If there is a legitimate reason though, you need to find it and combat your weakness. Maybe the product you released just did not cut it or the market did not see the value in it that you had imagined. Perhaps, you have not made the importance of your product easily seen. The good news is you now have market research for the next products. Figure out the why, so you can figure out the how.

3.) Find ways on HOW to fix the problem —This, I believe, is the biggest task for the business owner. Once you have discovered the source of the problem, you then have to figure out how to solve it. It is an arduous task because, in most cases, it means that you have to begin again. Just like a mathematical equation, when you forget to add a minus to a figure from your question, you'll have to start from scratch and make sure you don't repeat the same mistake. It is also like that in the business world most times. And when you finally figure out the how, write it down. Write down ways to combat it so that you can overcome it and come back better than ever.

4.) Execution – You must execute your plan on a massive scale. Once you have put together your plans, dive into action head first. There is no time for self-pity. There are a lot of smart people with million-dollar ideas that could have changed the world, but they failed once and refused to execute again. More so, there are other people in the world who have the same idea as yours. So will you allow anyone to edge you out when you already have the available resources? If you want to succeed at it, you need to execute over and over and over until your idea, product, business, or story is at the level you wish it to be.

I want to share a story with you about two men that I think everyone can look up to in some way. If you are reading this, I am almost certain these two men have made an impression on your life in some form or another. The first man grew up in what some would consider a very dysfunctional family. His older brothers all ran away at young ages to escape being around their father. He lied about his age so that he could get out of the house at an early age and become an ambulance driver during WWI. At the age of 22, he was fired from a newspaper company for lack of creativity and opened his own business. Shortly after, he experienced a bankruptcy and lost what little he did have. He left his home town and headed to Los Angeles with 40 dollars in order to pursue his backup plan, a career as a Hollywood actor... That never happened. At the first sign of success, he decided to build a home for his aging parents in California so that they could be closer to him.

Poor construction and failed attempts to make repairs ended in his mother dying one morning from carbon monoxide poisoning. This devastated him and set him back several years.

As business began to grow again, WWII struck and the United States Military took over his facility to repair tanks. The industry he was working in, everyone hated him because they thought what he was doing could be detrimental to the movie industry. Time and time again, he took blows and continued to fight back. Some of the amazing things he was quoted for saying include:

"All of our dreams can come true if we have the courage to pursue them."

"It's kind of fun to do the impossible."

And

"I only hope that we never lose sight of one thing – that it was all started by a mouse." – Mr. Walt Disney.

The second man is a little more recent and truly revolutionized modern-day technology. As a newborn, his parents gave him up for adoption, and he was placed in the system completely nameless. As an infant, he was adopted and did not know his biological family until he was 27 years old. Before he found his success, he traveled the road of failure. After dropping out of college, he backpacked around India with hardly any money, heavily using LSD and smoking marijuana. He slept in abandoned buildings and got dysentery, which caused him to lose 40 lbs. that he did not have to lose. In a biography of him, they tell the story of when he was sleeping in a dry river bed with a friend, when a thunder storm struck. The river bed quickly rushed with water, almost killing him and his friend. The goal was to make it to the Himalayas. Someone stole his ID and what little money he had, forcing him to come home to the States.

Once home, after several other failures, he founded his company and saw some success. After a few mistakes and setbacks, he saw the writing on the wall and resigned from the company he helped found before the board could vote and he could be fired. After several other failures, he came back to the original company he help found, and skyrocketed it to become the incredible company it is today.

He has been quoted for saying:

"Sometimes life is going to hit you in the head with a brick. Don't lose faith."

"Innovation distinguishes between a leader and a follower."

"I want to put a ding in the universe." – Steve Jobs.

These men and many more have exercised an incredible amount of mental toughness. Toughness is necessary when striving for success. Would you come back from some of these failures to make your ding in the universe, or would you simply give up after failed attempts? I encourage you to seek inspiration in others' success and strive to make your ding.

CHAPTER VI
EXERCISES TO INCREASE YOUR MENTAL TOUGHNESS

Just as the organs of the body are revitalized when we engage in physical exercises, our mental organs also need to be improved upon through exercise. Exercise will then serve as a stimulant that will help you to make good decisions as well as go through stress easier. The advantages that one who exercises a lot has over one who doesn't exercise is obvious, same goes for those who have done mental exercises and those who haven't. Exercise isn't supposed to be easy; it is a painful process. The bodybuilder with hard abs and big muscles didn't just get it sitting down, eating pizza and hamburgers. He went through a rigorous process; sit ups, push-ups, weightlifting . . . Nothing in this world is free. If you want to exercise your mind, the process is sure to be rigorous as well.

1.) Take away your motivators – I want you to examine two scenarios:

A.) You wake up refreshed from your 8 hours of sleep, you go through your perfect morning routine, and head off to the gym before you start your work day. At the gym, you meet up with your personal trainer and you go over what the plan is for the day. You have all the top of the line equipment, and your trainer is on you, pushing you harder and harder.

B.) You have a crappy day in general at work. Your boss is on you all day about your productivity and you're stressed out of your mind. You have been taking your work home with you nightly and getting no more than 5 hours of sleep. After work, you head home, change your clothes, and head out into the Florida heat with some free weights and a jump rope, with no personal trainer.

In which scenario would you imagine that you would be more productive and get a better workout? I think most would agree that Option A is prime, and with the help of those motivators, we would see results much quicker. This, however, isn't a book on fitness; it's a book on mental toughness. So what am I getting at? Be honest with yourself. Option A sounds awesome, but if that is not an option, who would even put themselves through option B? It wouldn't take long before you started to tell yourself how bad it sucks and how nice a shower and the couch sounds. Would you continue with your workout or would you come to a mental agreement that one skipped workout won't hurt anything?

In order to strengthen your mental toughness, you need to remove your motivators and do what you don't want to do anyway. If you work out with music every time you work out, I encourage you to go without it every now and then. You will see your workout will be so much more difficult; it will take more mental toughness than normal to get through it. At this point, you're exercising your muscles and your mind. Your willpower is strengthened along with your biceps. You might find it interesting to realize that most of the things you're motivated to do by these 'motivators' are actually not new to you. They are mostly those options you've considered too risky to consider, and you've consequently sidelined them. Although, you need supportive people, mental exercising demands that you get firsthand experience doing it by yourself because someday, you might not have those persons near you.

2.) Do what you are horrible at – Do what sucks first and do it often. If it is something you are horrible at, likely you don't enjoy doing it. Regardless, it needs to be done, so by doing this, you are accomplishing several things. 1 – You are being productive. 2 – You will get better and more efficient with it, and 3 -You are exercising mental toughness and determination by making yourself complete the task first and often. This can play a huge role in sports and in the business world.

If you hate cold calls but it's something you need to do, make it your goal to make 10 more than you HAVE TO and make it your goal to have it done first. If you love making the 3-point shot, but you can't make a lay up to save your life, then work on your lay ups.

3.) Guard your thoughts – No one knows your thoughts but you. Keep yourself accountable for them. It is called MENTAL toughness; it is directly related to your thoughts. How you think is how you will feel. If thoughts of weakness and/or excuses come into your mind, shut them down immediately. Your thoughts are a loaded firearm. If used correctly, they can save your life; if used in a negative manner, it can take your life. Be accountable and put the negative thoughts down now. Making this part of your routine will not only make you a more positive person, but it increases your mental toughness.

4.) Give up bad habits – We all have bad habits that we need to kick, some worse than others. Every bad habit has the potential to destroy our lives and, of course, our business. A thing is regarded as 'bad' because of that reason. The secret here is to make the decision and cut it out of your life immediately. When we "quit smoking" or whatever other habit 100 times a month, we are constantly giving ourselves a loss for that day. Once you have one bad habit you don't want to give up, nothing will really change. Take for example, someone who drinks to stupor every day. How much savings/investments will he be able to make compared with someone who doesn't spend too much money on drinks? There will be clear cut differences, I believe. You must understand that bad habits are like termites. They do not destroy with one quick jab. It is a gradual process of destruction.

If you tell yourself you quit and the next day you pick it up, you lost. If you do this to yourself over and over, regardless if you notice it, you are deteriorating your willpower and your mental toughness. We all have our bad habits we need to kick. Recognize them and work on them.

5.) Embrace good habits – I believe that, immediately after dropping a bad habit, you need to embrace a good one. If you don't, you might leave a big void behind which is a bad idea. To then fill the void of a bad habit, good habits should be cultivated. Set a daily routine and stick to it. You will despise it at first, but things will slowly get easier, and trust me, you will begin to like it. It might be really difficult to replace alcohol with water or to reduce your sleep hours from 8 to 6, but you will get into it with time. After all, the habits that are exercised are also developed over time. So, you should give yourself enough time to adapt to the new changes. Set your alarm for earlier than you care to wake up. When you get up, be productive; don't just sit on the couch when there is a long list of things you could accomplish with your early hours: read a book, write a book, pray, meditate on your thoughts, work out. . . Do something that is good for you, that you don't necessarily want to do. This progresses your physical body and your mental toughness. Routines are great and increase your productivity all the way around.

6.) Use Self-Talk – Who cares if the person next to you thinks you have lost your mind. Self-Talk is an incredible exercise to keep you on track. I have used this my entire life, and it really does help. Athletes use this when running, lifting weights, pushing themselves to the limit.

I once read somewhere that a man's explanation for speaking to himself while walking is: I love talking to a smart man, and I like hearing a smart man speak! That's incredible :). Why not make it even better by talking to a successful and mentally tough man/women when you feel like it?

When you get tired or when you feel like giving up, remind yourself how strong you are. Remind yourself you did not start the task to quit. Say it out loud. By vocalizing it, you're forcing yourself to hear it also. Scream it if necessary, and you will see that it will give you that extra boost of mental toughness you need to finish what you're doing. Once you finish whatever it is you set out to do, you will have strengthened your mental toughness and your body.

Just like your body takes time to transform, your mind is a muscle and needs time to transform as well. Don't expect to make the above changes and be a mental ninja in a week. Becoming mentally tough and staying that way is a life long journey.

7.) Try multitasking — Your brain can perform much more than you think, and in a perfect competition, you will have to multitask your brain to a maximum level. This does not necessarily mean that you overwork your brain; it only means that you allow your brain to spread out of its monotonous confinement. It helps a lot when you have different things to do at the same time because you will not get bored doing the same thing when there are many other options. "Monotony kills the interest."

8.) Visualize your success — Apart from flexing your muscles in front of the mirror every day and telling yourself just how bad you are over and over again, you should also try to IMAGINE what you are running after. Picture how great it's going to be to wake up like a CEO: You get the day's newspaper already folded on the table with a hot cup of coffee, wear the latest pants and shirts with matching shoes to your well-furnished office, being driven to the office in that Rolls Royce you've always dreamed of . . . Stop! Where are you? Still in that apartment building where you've lived for the past four years? You let the prospect of success drive you at full speed; it's all good.

CHAPTER VII
LEGITIMATE EXCUSES

There are none....

CHAPTER VIII
THE AFTERGLOW

While the broad theme I have discussed so far in this book is mental toughness, I want to stress the idea of success as I draw the curtains from here, since the reason I emphasized toughness is that I want it to stimulate you to become successful. Success is subjective, truly. But I would use these few remaining pages to explain to you my idea of success. Like failure, success is in stages. You can't see a Harvard graduate who hasn't been to high School. It is a little success that qualifies you for a great success. Success is relative. But nonetheless, success is success.

Imagine a young boy attending boxing classes. When he puts on the gloves and start to throw combos at the punching bag, he feels like a champion, like a young Muhammed Ali or a Floyd Mayweather. Or when the boy successfully knocks out an opponent, are happiness and accomplishments not what he feels? Yet, that is not the real success he dreams of. He wants to be a world champ, a national and international phenomenon, a legend of the sport . . . Well, let's assume he eventually becomes who he wants to be, a great boxer. Then there is another question I would ask: What else? He accomplished his goals, then what happened next? I want you to bear in mind that no story actually has an end; everyone stops wherever they feel comfortable. The whole world is a story that has not ended yet. This last chapter, therefore, in a bid to answer these questions, is based on managing success and being a better person than you were the day before.

Two businesses may come into prominence and limelight at relatively the same time, yet from history, we can see that one might enjoy the glitz and glamour for a short time while the other goes on to become bigger and bigger. There are many factors that contribute to the betterment or otherwise of any business's or person's continuity of success, but the most important thing that tells how long or short success will be is the management. How do you manage your success, so it won't be upside down at some point? I have a list of things you could put into practice once you've attained those great heights.

1. Never forget your failures — Your life is and will continue to be a record of failures and success. As it has been highlighted earlier that failures come before success, let me also say here that failure can come after success too. To prevent that from happening, the first thing to put into your head is the memory of your years of failures. Those days you've spent drafting plans that you'll later have to toss away. Those times when your proposals get constantly rejected and you keep getting

disappointing e-mails and feedback. . . Never forget how hard you suffered before you succeeded. Let that be your first step into managing your newfound success.

2. Look forward to higher heights — There is always a mountain after a mountain. There is always a place better than where you are. Your goal should be to better your success. Think progress. Think greater success. In the business world, you only have two moves: forward and backward. You can't stay in the same spot. If you attempt to stay in the same spot, others will overtake you in no time and you'll find yourself behind too soon. So to ensure your success is continuous, the last thing you need is complacency. Think progress. If you have succeeded in one city, what about expanding your business to other cities? It's another step to a good management of your success. Don't feel satisfied with where you are right now; there are better places you can be.

3. Build a team around you or your business — As your enterprise grows, you need to build a formidable team around you to make things easier. One of the side

effects of success is that, most times, you might not be able to handle it alone. So when that time comes, you need to build a team around you that can be given the responsibility of helping you with the management of your business. Everyone that works with or under you is important. A strong team is one where respect is accorded to everyone. Everyone in your company deserves adequate respect and encouragement, from your cleaner to your manager. Once everyone is made to understand the way the company is being run, it will be easier to progress with your business.

4. Don't boast about your success — Yeah, you have sworn to do some really nasty things to everyone who doubted how far you can actually go. You've really imagined how you'd stuff your success down their throats with disdain. My humble advice to you, when you finally cracked it, is that you should eat humble pie. As part of your mental strength, you should be able to resist some things, and boasting should be one of those things. You don't need to pull up in the latest designers just to prove you've made it big. You don't need to show off your jewelry on Instagram just to alert

everyone of your progress. A mentally tough person has nothing to prove.

5. Be a giver —I believe in this strongly. Giving is an important part of what tells how responsible you are. Every business feeds on the society we call market, and as such, they collect from the society. To be factual, giving back to the society is just as important if not more than getting from society. It should be part of your social responsibility. Our world is full of people who are helpless on their own; you might have been one of them and you've picked yourself up. The fact that you've successfully registered yourself as a successful man or woman doesn't mean you should never care for people who haven't made it as far as you have. Don't claim you made it on your own. You didn't. Someone believed in you and gave you a chance. Someone took the risk of striking a deal with you. Someone bought your product, so you should try to help someone too.

6. Appreciate other people's effort — When you mention Microsoft or Facebook, our mind immediately goes to the CEOs Bill Gates and Mark Zuckerberg. These great

companies have, no doubt, made their mark in the digital world. When you look deeper into these great companies, there are thousands of people who are making sure things work out well. There are many people who are contributing or have contributed one way or another to make your business a success, and it is expected of you to give due credits to them. When you refuse to appreciate other people's effort in your success, you might never get the support of others when you need it. Often times when people look at SoniSafe they see me as the fore front but in all honesty, I wouldn't have been able to make it a quarter of this far without several other people helping me along the way. From monetary to emotional support I needed it all and A LOT of it :)

7. Never stop thinking — When you were zero and you had nothing to show for yourself, you had only one thing that no one else can steal, and that's your thoughts. Now you've successfully turned those thoughts into progress. Now that you have many things at your disposal with which you can transform dreams to reality, you shouldn't stop dreaming. You shouldn't stop thinking. You should think more on how to better

what you are already doing, as well as bring more solutions to a confused world.

8. Stay simple — If we would begin writing the ordeals of superstars and business acumen that went from grace to grass in no time because of ridiculous living, we would need to write a whole new book. Success is hard to maintain, and a wise choice you can make in handling your success is to be simple. Besides that, success brings you to a position that makes you an influencer to others. Many people would want to be like you, and you must make a positive impact on their lives by being a good example.

We are all on our own journey, and your idea of success may differ extremely from mine or any other person's. Success does not necessarily relate to money, cars, and big houses. Success is just like beauty; it is in the eye of the beholder. Whatever your definition of success is, your level of mental toughness will correlate directly with rather or not you achieve that level. Show me a successful person that hasn't failed, and

I'll show you an ostrich with horns . . . They simply don't exist. Successful people strive through failure. If everything you're doing is routine and easy, and you aren't struggling at something, then you aren't growing. I encourage you to live outside your comfort zone, push yourself to greatness, and embrace failure. Fear of failure has kept genius men and women from accomplishing what they were meant to accomplish.

I would rather live my entire life broke and hustling, dreaming for more than to accept an average life and die with the unknown. Regret reaches everyone the level of it its greatness is what will make you mad. Success is hard but sucking at life is a horrible alternative.

Use this book as a guide, adopt these exercises in your life, and you will see the difference it makes in an incredibly short amount of time. I believe that someone reading this has the protentional to change lives, to make a difference in the world we live in today. Don't give up on your dreams; chase them until you reach them. We have one life to live; live it with conviction.

If you made it this far, lets connect. I truly appreciate your support in purchasing this book and allowing me to spread my message of mental resilience. If you purchased this book from Amazon or another online retailer, I would greatly appreciate an honest review on what you thought of the book. This will help me spread my message and critique my writings.

Feel free to reach out to me at Mtucker@ntactsecurity.com or contact me through my contact page on the website www.MitchellRTucker.com

CPSIA information can be obtained
at www.ICGtesting.com
Printed in the USA
LVHW110842111119
636959LV00009B/3600/P

9 780578 566146